THE
FIRST STEP

for People in Relationships with Sex Addicts

Mic Hunter, M.S., M.A., C.C.D.C.R., L.P.
and
Jem, a recovering codependent

CompCare®Publishers
Minneapolis, Minnesota 55441

© 1989 Mic Hunter
All rights reserved.
Published in the United States
by CompCare Publishers.

Library of Congress Cataloging-in-Publication Data

Hunter, Mic.
   The first step for people in relationships with sex addicts/Mic Hunter and Jem.
     p. cm.
   ISBN 0-89638-163-3; $3.95
   1. Sexual addiction. 2. Interpersonal relations. 3. Co-dependence (Psychology)
I. Jem. II. Title.
RC560.S43H86 1989
616.85'83—dc20   89-15709
                                               CIP

Cover design by Jeremy Gale
Interior design by Susan Rinek

Inquiries, orders, and catalog requests should be addressed to:

CompCare Publishers
2415 Annapolis Lane
Minneapolis, MN 55441
Call toll free 800/328-3330
(Minnesota residents, 612/559-4800

5	4	3	2	1
93	92	91	90	89

Contents

Please read this first

A Note from the Publisher

■

Following publication of two of the first books on sex addiction—*Out of the Shadows* (1983) and *Hope and Recovery* (1987)—and further growth of specialized Twelve Step groups for sex addicts, one thing has become very clear: in the life of almost every sex addict is a codependent person in need of information, reassurance, and help. This workbook was developed to fill a real and immediate need for information and to provide a life line for codependents who are involved in Twelve Step Programs of recovery or who want to learn more about the Twelve Step process.

This workbook has been designed to guide codependents through the challenging but absolutely *vital* First Step of a Twelve Step recovery program: *acknowledging the elements of powerlessness and unmanageability in their own lives.*

The book you are about to work through represents a true collaborative effort. A professional therapist (Mic Hunter) and Jem, a recovering codependent with more than five years of recovery, worked together to develop this resource based on an adaptation of the Twelve Step Program of Alcoholics Anonymous. Both share information and insights in the text to clarify the purpose and process of First Step work.

Using portions of Jem's life experience as background, these questions lead codependents through a self-exploration that will help them understand the roots, effects, and current realities of powerlessness and unmanageability in their lives.

A Note from the Authors

■

The First Step of the Twelve Step Program is the key to recovery. Without a full understanding and personalization of the First Step, the remaining eleven steps are crippled and seriously weakened. We recommend that you read the following items in order to build a good foundation for your First Step work:

- Chapter Five ("How It Works") in *Alcoholics Anonymous*
- Step One in *Twelve Steps and Twelve Traditions*
- "Jean's Story" in *Hope and Recovery*

(For further information on these publications, see the Recommended Reading section on page 121.)

The Twelve Steps of
Alcoholics Anonymous

1. We admitted we were powerless over alcohol—that our live had become unmanageable.

2. Came to believe that a Power greater than ourselves could restore us to sanity.

3. Made a decision to turn our will and our lives over to the care of God *as we understood Him.*

4. Made a searching and fearless moral inventory of ourselves.

5. Admitted to God, to ourselves, and to another human being the exact nature of our wrongs.

6. Were entirely ready to have God remove all these defects of character.

7. Humbly asked Him to remove our shortcomings.

8. Made a list of all persons we had harmed, and became willing to make amends to them all.

9. Made direct amends to such people wherever possible, except when to do so would injure them or others.

10. Continued to take personal inventory, and when we were wrong, promptly admitted it.

11. Sought through prayer and meditation to improve our conscious contact with God, *as we understood Him,* praying only for knowledge of His will for us and the power to carry that out.

12. Having had a spiritual awakening as the result of these steps, we tried to carry this message to alcoholics, and to practice these principles in all our affairs.

The Twelve Steps
Adapted for Codependents to Sex Addicts

1. We admitted we were powerless over codependency to sex addiction—that our lives had become unmanageable.

2. Came to believe that a Power greater than ourselves could restore us to sanity.

3. Made a decision to turn our will and our lives over to the care of God as we understood God.

4. Made a searching and fearless moral inventory of ourselves.

5. Admitted to God, to ourselves, and to another human being the exact nature of our wrongs.

6. Were entirely ready to have God remove all these defects of character.

7. Humbly asked God to remove our shortcomings.

8. Made a list of all persons we had harmed, and became willing to make amends to them all.

9. Made direct amends to such people wherever possible, except when to do so would injure them or others.

10. Continued to take personal inventory and when we were wrong, promptly admitted it.

11. Sought through prayer and meditation to improve our conscious contact with God, as we understood God, praying only for knowledge of God's will for us and the power to carry that out.

12. Having had a spiritual awakening as the result of these steps, we tried to carry this message to others, and to practice these principles in all our affairs.

Mic's
Introduction

Sex addiction and codependency: the words are relatively new; the problems they refer to are not. Through the years, millions of people have struggled with difficulties directly and indirectly related to obsessive sexual thoughts and compulsive sexual behaviors. It is only in recent years, however, that these problems have been identified and treated as forms of addiction and codependency. Subsequently, the Twelve Step Program of Alcoholics Anonymous was adapted for the special needs and problems of sex addicts and codependents to sex addicts. As with alcoholism, eating disorders, and other compulsive behaviors, the Twelve Steps have proven very useful in helping sex addicts and codependents recover and live productive, meaningful, self-respecting, and peaceful lives.

Prior to beginning your First Step work in this book, it will be useful for you to review some key concepts.

Sex Addiction

Sex addiction refers to the thinking and behavior patterns of a person who uses sex to cope with life and to defend against low self-worth and a shameful identity. For the addict, sex is not a fulfilling experience that enhances a primary relationship and life itself, but a compulsive, often highly ritualized activity that ultimately adds to the pain and loneliness the addict is already battling. There are several characteristics that are commonly seen in individuals who are addicted to sex:

Loss of control—A person addicted to sex is unable to comfortably eliminate or modify for any significant period of time the sexual or sexualized behaviors and thoughts that are creating problems in his or her life. An example of loss of control would be the following: Due to physical and emotional discomfort related to compulsive masturbation, an individual sets up a rule that he or she will masturbate once or twice a week and only at home, yet the very next day, this individual modifies that rule to allow for weekly masturbation at work or in the car; the next day, the rule is further modified; a few days later, the rule is broken completely. People who are struggling with loss of control often set very specific rules in an attempt to demonstrate to themselves and/or to others that they are not addicted. Subsequently, they change the rules to keep pace with their behaviors. Essentially, the behavior begins to determine the rule, rather than the rule determining the behavior.

Preoccupation—A sex addict is likely to evidence a limited attention span or even complete inattentiveness to people, things, and concepts other than sex. In the sex addict's view of the world, nearly everything is somehow related to the object of his or her addiction. The progressive nature of addiction combines with preoccupation leading the person to become highly focused—obsessed, really—with thoughts of obtaining new sexual highs.

Progression—There is a tendency for the sex addict, over time, to add to the range of his or her sexual behavior and to increase the frequency of the behavior as well. An example of progression: Let's say that a person begins purchasing pornographic literature on a rather casual basis—when he or she thinks of it, perhaps once a month.

If that person is addicted, this single activity and its frequency soon will not be sufficient for the person to obtain the desired effect or high. Subsequently, the person purchases increasingly more graphic material on a more regular basis—first monthly, then weekly, then twice a week.

Highly developed and active defense mechanisms—No one enjoys the feeling of being out of control. Therefore, when a person is, in fact, experiencing a chronic loss of control, he or she is likely to utilize one or more well developed psychological defense mechanisms so as to avoid conscious comprehension of the realities and consequences of the situation.

Repression is a defense mechanism that essentially blocks painful memories so that a person is not consciously aware of them. Unfortunately, this defense mechanism interferes with a person's ability to identify problematic patterns and learn from his or her own life experiences.

Denial is a defense mechanism that makes a person unwilling or unable to acknowledge that an event has a negative effect. For example, a client of mine who is a sex addict described to me how he would leave his place of employment during breaks and drive around the immediate neighborhood looking for street prostitutes. My client vehemently *denied* that he was fearful when he was doing this, even though the police were cracking down and making numerous arrests for prostitution in the area. He also knew that if he were to be arrested for solicitation, he would be placing his family and his political career in great jeopardy. Still, this man steadfastly maintained that the rapid breathing and sweaty palms he experienced as he cruised the neighborhood were only signs of being "high" and sexually stimulated, not physical symptoms of fear. This man did not deny what he was doing; he *did* deny that what he was doing was affecting him negatively.

Minimization is a defense mechanism wherein a person acknowledges that something is taking place, but discounts or shrinks its importance and/or the importance of its probable consequences. The sex addict who cruises neighborhoods for prostitutes during his coffee breaks might say *"I guess I could get arrested, but they're not that vigilant in that neighborhood. Besides, I'd never get fired for a little adventure like that; it's just not that big a deal."*

Rationalization is a defense mechanism that essentially fixes blame for an occurrence or behavior on another person or some external event or circumstance. An example of this would be the person who acknowledges his or her extramarital affairs, knows they're wrong, but justifies the behavior because of travel and frequent separations, poor communication with a spouse, or refusal of a spouse to participate in certain sexual activities.

Codependency

Codependency refers to the thinking and behavior patterns of a person who focuses on other people (usually one other person) to cope with life and to defend against low self-worth and a shameful identity. There are several characteristics that are commonly found in people who are codependent, in this case codependent to sex addicts.

Loss of control—Codependent people erroneously believe that they somehow have the ability to control the behaviors of others. Of course, one person cannot *really* control another person, but that fact doesn't stop the codependent from continuing to try. The codependent is unable to comfortably eliminate or modify for any significant period of time thoughts and behaviors that are focused on other people.

Preoccupation—The codependent person spends much of his or her time thinking about other people, rather than about himself or herself. For example, consider the man I knew who was married to a sex addict: each time he'd look at a clock when he and his wife were not together, he would try to figure out where she would be at that time and if there was *any* chance that she could be having sex at that moment. His performance on the job understandably suffered because his mind was constantly focused on his wife and her possible activities, rather than on his job-related tasks.

Progression—Eventually, more and more things in the codependent person's environment act as triggers for the person's thoughts and activities related to the sex addict.

Highly developed and active defense mechanisms—In many ways, the codependent and the sex addict think alike; they share similar belief systems and use the same defense mechanisms. These similarities may help to explain why codependents and sex addicts so often find each other and establish relationships.

The codependent person tends to use *repression* to enable himself or herself to overlook the self-defeating patterns he or she is stuck in. *("I don't remember that he had an affair the first year we were married.")* Many times, the codependent person doesn't even notice obvious similarities in his or her relationships and has one abusive relationship after another. The codependent person is likely to "forget" what happened the last time he or she was in a similar situation.

When someone points out to the codependent person the disrespectful and/or self-defeating patterns in his or her relationships, the defense mechanisms of *denial* and *minimization* may become operational, making it unlikely that the codependent will fully grasp the negative nature and consequence of these patterns. *(It* couldn't *have been her coming out of that motel with a man; he was working that afternoon." "Oh, every man plays around when he gets the chance; I'm just glad he still comes home to me at the end of his business trips.")*

Even when the codependent person does gain some insights into the negative relationship cycle he or she is caught up in, *rationalization* makes it possible for him or her to avoid responsibility and to avoid taking any action that will result in significant change. *("I don't blame him for getting bored with our sexual relationship; I'm too tired to respond to him as I should." "At least he isn't having an affair; those nude stage shows he's been going to more often lately seem to satisfy him.")*

As you respond to the questions in this workbook and, in effect, write your First Step history, be alert to your use of repression, denial, minimization, and rationalization. Although these defenses may have been somewhat useful to you earlier in your life, now they might actually *prevent* you from grasping the all-important First Step. It is so important to have more than an intellectual understanding of the First Step. In order to fully experience this Step and its effects, you need to grasp the concept of powerlessness and unmanageability *on an emotional level.* Therefore, as you respond to questions and write about your behaviors and thoughts in this workbook, I encourage you to *focus on your feelings*—then and now—and write about them as well.

Jem's
Introduction

The beginning of any Twelve Step recovery program focuses on the task of carefully looking at our lives by working the First Step. As codependents, our lives were in a shambles because of our behavioral patterns of establishing relationships with people addicted to sex. Regardless of the specific acting-out behaviors involved, we know that our lives have been profoundly affected by sex addicts and our relationships with them.

The sex addicts in our lives may have been fantasizing about sex to the extent that it was impossible for them to stay in touch with those around them, much less be emotionally available to those people. The sex addicts in our lives may have been preoccupied with the use of pornography, or with nude stage shows; they may have masturbated compulsively; they may have been unable to stop having affairs, despite many promises and vows to change their behavior. We know that sex addiction can lead to legal and medical problems. We also know firsthand that sex addiction can lead to significant losses: loss of physical and/or mental health, loss of careers, loss of financial security, loss of primary relationships.

Through their behaviors, sex addicts affect everyone around them, especially those of us who are closest to them. Certainly, sex addicts suffer the consequences of their behavior, but so do their children, other family members, friends, and those of us who are in primary relationships with them. As codependents, we try everything we can

think of to control the addict: we fight; we bargain; we with-
hold sex; we promise sex; we spy; we plead; we manipulate;
we try our best to satisfy the addict's needs and wants. And
why do we continue to try so hard to control the addict
when nothing seems to work? Because we are addicted *ourselves*—to the sex addicts in our lives. In fact, we came to
see that it was our *own* addiction that was making us crazy.
So many of us had tried to break the self-defeating cycle we
sensed we were in—many of us, in fact, tried to break this
cycle with more than one addict. Recovery asks us to stop
trying to control the sex addicts in our lives and to *focus on
ourselves instead.* The First Step asks us to become aware
that we, too, have an addiction in the form of codependency.
And, *like sex addicts we are also powerless.*

The Roots of Our Addiction

Looking at our early years, many of us codependents can
see the roots of our powerlessness there. Many of us find
parallels between how we were treated in our families as
children and the nature of the relationships we subsequently chose as adults. Some of us realize that we were
raised by parents who were addicted to sex, drugs, or self-
destructive behaviors. Some of us suffered sexual, physical,
or emotional abuse as children. When we look carefully at
our past and present lives, we can more clearly see how our
attempts to cope with abusive environments generated—if
not necessitated—certain patterns of thinking and behavior that would take the form of codependency later in our
lives. As adults, many of us continue to behave like the vul-
nerable, frightened children we were, rather than understanding and exercising the choices we now have as adults.

Approaching the First Step

Recovery from codependency to sex addiction can be a long
and rough road. The First Step asks us to look back over our

lives to see for ourselves how sexual addiction and codependency have affected us. The First Step also asks us to review the ways we have tried to control the addict(s) in our lives. When we see that *we do not have the power to stop the addict* (or even our own crazy behaviors) by ourselves, we will also see that our old ways do not work and that we need to make some changes.

The First Step asks us to look at two components of our addiction: *our powerlessness and our unmanageability*. *Powerlessness* is the inability to stop "acting out" or behaving in self-defeating and/or self-destructive ways. In the past, most of us made sincere promises to change. We made these promises to ourselves, to other people, and even to our God. But, before long, these promises were redefined, then broken completely. If we can accept that we have behaved irrationally as a result of codependency—not due to a lack of intelligence or a weak will—we will be able to reduce our shame and forgive ourselves for our mistakes. And when we do these things, we will find a new acceptance of ourselves and others. *Unmanageability* refers to the impact that our codependency has had *on all areas of our lives*. When we look at the aspect of unmanageability, we begin to see the terrible price we have paid for our acting-out behaviors. We may actually begin to grieve for all that we have given up or lost because of our intense focus on the sex addict(s) in our lives.

Our emotions actually help us begin the healing process, which is recovery. The First Step can be a very painful process, reminding us of past hurts and losses. At the same time, the First Step can be a very freeing adventure that helps us see that we can change and grow, that we are not trapped in destructive behavior patterns, and that we can live self-nurturing lives. Once we begin to understand that our actions were the result of our codependence, our shame loses its intensity and we begin to view ourselves as worthwhile people, fully capable of making healthier choices for ourselves and our lives. And when we begin to feel better about ourselves, our relationships become invigorating rather than draining, we seem to have more time for ourselves, and we can become truly intimate with those around us.

Not all of the questions in this workbook will apply to your situation or your experience. Nevertheless, take time to think through each of the questions posed and be as specific as possible in your answers. If a question doesn't quite fit for your situation, expand and individualize your response. *In order to get the most benefit from this workbook, focus on your feelings.*

As a codependent in my fifth year of recovery, I feel that it will be helpful—and also consistent with the sharing aspects of the Twelve Step Program—to include in this workbook portions of my own First Step, along with portions of my personal story and insights from other recovering codependents. As you move through the questions and read about the ways powerlessness and unmanageability affected my own life and the lives of other codependents, you may be better able to look closely at your own situation and write about it in a way that helps you see and accept your powerlessness on an emotional level. *Please note that my own story and First Step writings as well as the comments of other recovering codependents are printed in italics preceding most of the questions in this workbook.*

The First Step

Reviewing Childhood

As you review your childhood through the questions that follow, look carefully for experiences, behavior patterns, and beliefs that may have led to your powerlessness and unmanageability as an adult. No one is *born* codependent, but it seems quite clear that for many people, the codependent belief system begins in childhood, particularly if a child observes adults in his or her life exhibiting codependent behaviors.

In order to identify your basic beliefs about the way people "should" act, it is helpful to look at ways in which you may have been taught to be codependent. It will be easier to change your codependent behaviors if you can gain an understanding of how and why you interact with people the way you do. Remember, most of what we learn as children comes from observing people and how they behave, rather than listening to what they say. For example, the parent who says that it is important to be treated respectfully yet tolerates abuse, is essentially teaching his or her child that abuse is acceptable. *Simply stated, to the child observer-learner, behavior provides a more powerful and memorable lesson than words.* The primary purpose of this workbook section is to help you understand the roots of your codependency, not to help you identify and build a case against people who contributed to your codependent belief system and behaviors. Fixing blame is never a useful exercise.

Jem: "It is such a relief to discover that we are not born codependent; this adds to our hope for recovery."

■ **1.** How would you describe your relationships with your parents and other family members as you were growing up? Generally speaking, were these relationships characterized by feelings of: Love? Fear? Warmth? Anger?

"As a child, I never remember the subject of sex being discussed in our family. Instead, I learned about sex from a friend. Her mother was a nurse and she brought home educational pamphlets on the subject of sex. Years later, when I suggested that my mother tell my little sister about sex, she laughed at me and told me that I was just being silly."

■ **2.** How was the subject of sex discussed in your family? Who told you about sex? Does the manner in which this subject was handled tell you anything about the attitudes your family members had about sex?

"When my mother encountered me at a very young age exploring another child's body—playing 'doctor'— she reprimanded me in such a way that I never forgot the incident or the intense feelings of shame I had afterwards."

■ **3.** How did you first become aware of sex and your own sexuality? Were these early insights and experiences pleasant or unpleasant for you?

"*I can see so clearly now that by observing my mother's behavior and seeing the effects of her choices, I received two unmistakable messages from her that would stay with me for years: women are supposed to take care of men, and real women put the needs of others before their own needs.*"

■ **4.** What messages did you receive as a child about relationships—specifically male and female roles and "shoulds" within relationships? How have you followed or rebelled against these messages? Can you see ways in which these early messages relate to your codependency now?

■ **5.** How do you remember other people treating your body when you were a child? Were you made to feel ugly or beautiful? Did you get the sense that your body was to be covered up or shown?

"Even when I was still a young child, my father told me that I should grow my hair long and wear it over my breasts so they'd look bigger. When we went shopping for clothing together, he'd choose items of apparel for me that made me look much older than I was."

■ **6.** As a child, what kinds of messages did you receive about desired form of dress? Was it somehow communicated that you should dress to please yourself . . . or someone else?

"I received a clear message from members of my family that my body did not belong to me and that I was not old enough to know what I wanted or didn't want in terms of physical contact."

■ **7.** Were you in any way taught that your body did not belong to you? For example, were you not given the power to decide who could touch you and/or how?

■**8.** Did you have any traumatic experiences as a child? If so, how did you and other members of your family react to these experiences?

"When I was a child, I cried very easily in sad situations. And whenever I cried, my sister would taunt me and call me 'cry baby' and my mother would treat me with disgust and tell me to 'grow up.' "

■ **9.** How were you treated when you expressed emotions as a child? If possible, reflect back on a few specific experiences and describe them in as much detail as possible.

■**10.** Were you physically abused as a child? Who abused you? In what ways do you feel this abuse affected your attitudes about physical contact and relationships?

"When I was a young child, adult family members touched me inappropriately and forced me to kiss and hug them in ways that made me feel very uncomfortable."

■ **11.**   Were you sexually abused as a child? Who abused you? In what ways do you feel this abuse affected your attitudes about sex?

"After family members abused me, they often tried to 'make it up to me' in ways that I, as a child, perceived as positive attention. In fact, the attention I received in the aftermath of abuse represented the only times in my young life that I didn't feel ignored."

■ **12.** How were you treated following physical or emotional abuse? How did it make you feel?

"Very early in my life—even before adolescence—I was ridiculed by members of my family for not having boyfriends."

■ **13.** Was it directly or indirectly communicated to you that it was wrong, bad, or shameful to be without a close friend of the opposite sex? Were you somehow taught through the behavior and choices of others that your life was incomplete or that you could not fully exist without a boyfriend or girlfriend?

"As a child, I watched my mother stay with a number of spouses who were abusive to her and her children. The message I learned from this was that being with anyone was better than being alone."

■ **14.** Did you in any way learn through the behavior and choices of other people that an abusive relationship is better than no relationship at all?

■ **15.** Considering the behavior patterns characteristic of codependency, would you describe any member(s) of your childhood family as codependent? What kinds of addicts did this person (or these people) get into relationships with: Alcoholics? Sex addicts? Compulsive gamblers? Compulsive overeaters?

"I remember that the only recognition I got in my family was for the things I did for others. Basically, I was not encouraged to do things for myself."

■ **16.** What experiences, behaviors, and thought patterns in your childhood have contributed to your co-dependency as an adult?

"Looking back at my childhood years: I learned that I came to tolerate abuse. I learned that I did not have a sense of positive self-worth. I learned that being physical was frightening to me."

■ **17.** What have you learned about yourself and your codependency from looking back at your childhood years?

Remembering Adolescence

Adolescence is likely to be a time when the seeds of codependency planted in childhood take root in a person's life. The teenage years represent a stage of life when most people begin to think and learn about their own sexuality and the opposite sex.

Jem: "Adolescence is a trying time; we establish our identities more fully and we work through new feelings and insecurities about our sexuality. For many of us, it is the time of life when codependency begins to control our lives. As we look back, many of us are able to identify the fact that even during our earliest dating experiences, we were exhibiting codependent behaviors."

■ **18.** How did puberty begin for you? Was it early or late compared to your friends? How did you react to the onset of puberty?

■ **19.** How were you prepared for puberty? Who helped you understand and deal with the physical and psychological changes commonly associated with this time of life?

"I remember always being either shamed or ridiculed when I asked questions related to sex."

■ **20.** Who, if anyone, in your family did you talk with about subjects like menstruation, feelings of sexual arousal, personal hygiene, sexual dreams, and wet dreams? Generally, how were you responded to by members of your family when you asked questions about personal issues related to sexuality?

━━

"*I matured relatively late, and when I finally did reach puberty, my sister said 'it's about time.' Although I told my mother as soon as I started menstruating, she completely ignored the news. I was so emotionally numb by the time I was an adolescent that I honestly didn't realize that an important event in my life was being trivialized, if not completely overlooked.*"

■ **21.** How did your parents and other family members react to the onset of your puberty?

■ **22.** What, if anything, did members of your family say about your changing body? How did you feel about what was said?

"I put so much time and energy into my relationships with boys that I had no resources left for friendships with girls."

■ **23.** As an adolescent, how did you interact with people of your same sex? How is the nature of this interaction similar to and/or different from the way you relate as an adult with people of your same sex?

*"I remember always feeling such an intense longing.
I just wanted to be special to some boy."*

■ **24.** As an adolescent, how did you interact with people of the opposite sex? How is this interaction similar to and/or different from the way you interact as an adult with people of the opposite sex?

■ **25.** At what age did you begin dating and what feelings did you have about your first dates?

"I was such a pleaser—always so deferential to boys, always so cooperative—that I lost sight of who I was and what I really wanted."

■ **26.** What kinds of people did you date? How would you describe the people you dated and how do you think they would have described you?

■ **27.** In what ways were the people you dated early in your life similar to and/or different from the partner(s) you've had or have as an adult?

"As I grew older, I had specific questions and concerns about sex. But a rational discussion of such things was out of the question in our family—there was so much shame attached to the subject of sex and everything related to it."

■ **28.** How were subjects such as dating, sexual activity, and birth control discussed by members of your family?

"My first sexual experience with a boyfriend meant to me that finally someone cared enough to focus his attention exclusively on me for a time; this attention translated to some faint glimmers of self-worth."

■ **29.** Did you have sex for the first time as an adolescent? If so, how and when did sexual activity begin for you? What was your first sexual experience like? Describe the feelings you remember having about this experience then . . . and now. How were your early sexual experiences similar to and/or different from the sexual experiences you've had as an adult?

*"In my relationships with the boys I dated, I was sub-
missive to the point that I completely denied my own
feelings and needs."*

■ **30.** As an adolescent, were you active or passive regarding sexual behaviors?

■**31.** Did you use/abuse alcohol and other drugs as an adolescent? If so, how did your use of chemicals affect your sexual behavior?

"While everyone else was planning careers and families, I was obsessed with pleasing my current boyfriend and doing whatever I felt was necessary to make sure that he'd never leave me."

■ **32.**   As an adolescent, what did you imagine your future would be like in terms of career, relationships, a family of your own?

"I feel very sad when I look at my adolescent years and realize that my loneliness, shame, and low self-esteem led to a path of codependency that I would not depart from for years."

■**33.** What have you learned about yourself and your codependency from looking back at your teenage years? What feelings do these memories conjure up for you?

Applying the First Step to Our Adult Lives

Now that you have worked through a history of the earlier years of your life, you are better prepared to see how the First Step can be worked most effectively in your adult life. Essentially, the First Step asks three questions:

- Have you tried everything you can think of to control the sex addict(s) in your life?
- Were your efforts to control the sex addict(s) in your life effective?
- How painful for you is the way you are living now?

Working through the First Step and grasping its significance in your adult life on an emotional level can be a frightening and painful experience. For this reason, pay particularly close attention to the presence of those highly developed and active defense mechanisms summarized on pages 3–6. It truly would be unfortunate if you allowed repression, denial, minimization, and/or rationalization to obstruct your First Step work and your recovery.

Jem: "When you've accepted the First Step on an emotional level, your resistance to do those things required to recover will almost disappear. This acceptance is an extremely powerful and freeing experience. Following a look back at the past, we are then in a better position to determine our readiness to accept the wisdom of the First Step. This all-important step in recovery addresses two primary elements in our lives: powerlessness and unmanageability."

Powerlessness

The thirty-seven questions that follow in this section relate to the element of powerlessness in the codependent's life.

"Powerlessness was, for me, an inability to consistently choose healthy behaviors because of my obsession with my partner and my ongoing efforts to control his behavior."

■ **34.** What does powerlessness mean to you?

"I believe that my powerlessness manifested itself in my craving for sugar, in my fears that my partner would leave me, in my overall fear of sex, and in my obsession with keeping my partner focused on me."

■ **35.** What thoughts and behaviors have you been powerless over in your life?

■**36.** How would you define sex addiction?

*"When I think about it, I believe that three people in my
life were addicted to sex: my father, my very first boyfriend, and my current partner."*

■ **37.** How many sex addicts have there been in your
life? What was—or is—your relationship with each of
them?

■**38.** How would you define codependency to sex addiction?

"As a mature adult and a recovering codependent, I have become much more comfortable with my body. For years, I focused on my feelings that my breasts were too small; I even investigated implant surgery for the purpose of enlarging my breasts. At the same time, I was afraid that if my breasts were larger, I'd attract too much attention."

■ **39.** Are you comfortable with your body? Do you focus your thoughts and concerns on perceived inadequacies of your body—particularly your sex organs?

"*Prior to my awareness of and recovery from codependency, I was a cigarette smoker and lived on sugary snacks, which resulted in daily headaches. Now, in recovery, I belong to a health club, I eat better foods, I am watchful of my overall health, and I've stopped smoking.*"

■**40.** How important is it to you that you take good care of your body? Are you regularly attentive to exercise, nutrition, personal hygiene, and health maintenance?

"I knew that prior to meeting me, my partner had dated a woman with long red hair. Although I had never worn my hair long and didn't particularly want to, I grew it long and dyed it red, hoping that this would make it less likely that my partner would leave me for a redhead."

■**41.** What *don't* you like about your physical appearance? Are there specific things that your partner doesn't like about your physical appearance, and how do they relate to what you dislike about yourself? What have you tried to change about yourself?

"Even though I wasn't comfortable in sexy lingerie and seductive 'costumes,' I used to buy these items of apparel and wear them because I was convinced that I wasn't sexy enough for my partner just being me."

■**42.** Do you dress in ways that make you feel uncomfortable or unnatural to please your partner and/or to attempt to control him or her?

"Prior to my recovery, I always preferred to remain fully (and unprovocatively) clothed in front of my partner when we were home alone together; I did this out of fear that he would want to have sex with me because I had 'enticed' him with my manner of dress."

■ **43.** When you are with your partner, how comfortable are you without clothing on? Do you consciously dress in such a way that you cannot be accused of "enticing" your partner?

"*As a codependent to a sex addict, I erroneously thought that I could control his addiction with my own efforts and behavior. I felt that having sex with my partner was the best way—perhaps the only way—to insure that he wasn't having sex with someone else.*"

■ **44.** In your relationship with your partner, have you used sexual activity and/or the withholding of sexual activity to manipulate, punish, or otherwise control your partner? Write about some of the ways you have attempted to do this.

"It seems to me that whenever I was open with my partner about anything—whether it involved our relationship or not—I would ask him to hold and comfort me. During these times, he would inevitably begin touching me in a sexual way. Even if I wasn't interested in having sex at those times, I always felt that I should be sexual with him to 'repay' him for comforting me."

■ **45.** Have you "settled" for sex at times when you really wanted something else from your partner? Write about what you really wanted (and needed) at those times.

"In many ways, it was always very difficult for me to feel close to my partner. But this was my logic: at least when I was having sex with him, I knew I had his attention. When he'd return home from trips, I'd always suggest that we have intercourse immediately. I now believe this ritual was my way of making sure that we still had a relationship and that I was in his thoughts during the time he was gone. We'd usually have a fight after we had intercourse, then he'd go away and pout. He wouldn't talk to me until we had sex again, which I would initiate in an effort to end the silence and in some way close the distance between us."

■ **46.** Have you used sex to accomplish one or more of the following things: To reassure yourself of your partner's attentiveness? To patch up a fight? To initiate conversation that otherwise would not take place? Describe a couple of incidents in which you used sex in an attempt to control your partner's behavior.

"I felt that in order to hold my partner's interest, I had to be willing to try anything and everything. In order to feel as though I had at least some control over what was going to happen, I would often make suggestions of new sexual things to try—even when they didn't appeal to or interest me at all. Looking back, many co-dependents realize that they pretended to enjoy things, even when they didn't."

■ **47.** Have you lied—to yourself, to your partner, and/ or to others—about your feelings concerning your sex life and specific sexual activities? Cite examples of times when you have lied in this way and write about the reasons you think you did this.

*"When I posed for photographs to be published in a por-
nographic magazine, I felt shameful. But there was
such conflict inside of me: I actually felt guilty when I
changed my mind and asked my partner not to allow
the photos to be published."*

■ **48.** Have you engaged in sexual activities that are in-
consistent with your preferences, judgment, moral
standards or beliefs? What feelings do you associate
with having done these things: Anger? Shame? Guilt?
Sadness?

"*I would have to get drunk in order to do something I was uncomfortable doing, such as when we—as a couple—were sexual with another person.*"

■ **49.** Have you relied on mood-altering chemicals in order to do something of a sexual nature that you otherwise wouldn't do? If so, how do you feel about this?

"I usually tried to have pre-arranged plans with other people on the weekends, and I took classes at night during the week so that it would be practically impossible (from the standpoint of time, if nothing else) for him to ask me for sex."

■ **50.** Have you tried to limit your partner's access to you for sexual activity by being compulsively busy, or finding reasons to leave home, or falling asleep? Think about it: have you structured your life in this way consciously or subconciously?

■**51.** What circumstances usually make you want to say no to having sex: Being concerned about other responsibilities? Feeling angry or afraid? Being extremely tired, or ill, or in physical pain? In these circumstances, how difficult is it for you to follow through and say no to your partner? How do you feel when you *do* say no to sex for a specific reason?

"In order to get out of having sex with my partner, I used to make excuses saying that I had other things to do; or I'd say yes to him, then conveniently forget. In recovery, I'm getting better at saying no for whatever reason is legitimate to me. Now my partner knows that when I say yes to sex, I really mean it."

■ **52.** When you *do* say no to sex, do you make excuses and/or indirectly say no or do you respond directly? How do you feel when you say no?

"The few times I did say no to sex, he became extremely angry with me and began listing all of my faults. In fact, he wouldn't stop picking on me until I agreed to have sex with him. These scenes were so unpleasant that I finally gave up refusing him; I concluded that saying no to him wasn't worth the price I had to pay."

■ **53.** What has happened when you have said no to sex with your partner? What did your partner do and say to you when you refused and how did it make you feel?

"Oftentimes, I would stay up late at night watching television, just hoping that he would go to bed without me and that he'd be asleep when I finally got to bed. Then, when I got into bed, I'd be extremely careful not to wake him so he wouldn't try to have sex with me."

■ **54.** Have you used certain activities, behaviors, or rituals to avoid having sex with your partner? If so, try to recall some specific examples.

"I used to wake up to find my partner touching me sexually. At first, I allowed him to have sex with me while I fell back to sleep. This was an easy way to give him what I thought he needed, without having to do much of anything myself. In time, though, I felt that I was being violated and used in these circumstances because I had not consented to have sex with him."

■**55.** Does your partner have sex with you when you are asleep or ill? How do you feel about this?

"In the past, I felt so distant from my partner as well as from myself during sex. I simply didn't want to pay attention to my feelings of loneliness and pain. But now, when we're both working our recovery programs, sex has become an expression of the closeness and intimacy that we feel toward one another and within our relationship."

■**56.** How close and intimate do you feel toward your partner while you are engaged in sexual activity with him or her?

"I never believed that who I was or what I did sexually was good enough for my partner. To my way of thinking, I was never cute enough or skinny enough or feminine enough; I also worried that I was too bitchy, too emotional, and too demanding for him to want to stay with me."

■**57.** Do you feel that you are an adequate sex partner?

"Each time I did have sex with my partner, my mind would automatically wander. I'd think about errands that I needed to run or things I needed to shop for. This distraction somehow helped me to avoid a painful reality: that my partner and I only connected physically and not emotionally and that in many ways, I was being used by him."

■**58.** While engaged in sex with your partner, are you preoccupied with other things? While having sex, do you automatically think of things that will distract you from the activity and your feelings regarding it?

———

*"Before recovery, I was so preoccupied with my part-
ner's wants and needs that I was completely out of
touch with my own wants and needs. It took me a long
time to recognize and understand what I did and did
not enjoy, sexually and otherwise. But I was reluctant
to express myself and I was really afraid to set any
kind of limits with my partner because I thought he
would find me difficult and/or boring. Now, in recovery, I am able to fully express my wants, needs, and
limitations—both before and during sex."*

■ **59.** In what ways are you able and unable to express
your needs—emotional and sexual—to your partner?

"Although I had no interest in doing so, I used to go to porno theaters with my partner. I did this in a desperate attempt to keep him interested in me."

■ **60.** Have you done things you aren't interested in or perhaps even object to in an effort to keep your partner interested in you? If so, list a few of the things you have done and how you felt about doing them at the time.

*"Now, in recovery, one way that I can tell when I'm tak-
ing part in healthy sex is that my emotions and my
body are in agreement with my desire to have sex. I
have come to see that when I was acting out, I was focused only on my partner and that I was completely
ignoring my own desires."*

■ **61.** How would you define healthy sex?

"Early in recovery, when I began setting sexual limits in my relationships, I was torn between the way I wanted to be and the way I had been for so many years. It seemed as if nothing I did was right. I thought I might be crazy. In fact, I often hoped that I was crazy. My faulty logic went like this: if I was insane, then I wasn't responsible for the choices I had made and, therefore, I wouldn't have to change."

■ **62.**   Have you ever thought that you might be crazy? At the times you've had these thoughts, what was happening in your life?

"I had one therapist who never said a word to me; he just listened. When I think about that now, I feel angry that this therapist never pointed out to me how crazy my life was and how I was hurting myself with my behaviors. Another therapist I had pointed out to me the parallels between my family and my relationship with my partner. I believe that my understanding of the similarities between my relationship with my family and my partner actually signalled the beginning of my First Step work. My new understanding also helped me look at the sexual abuse I had suffered as a child. When I was in couples' therapy with my partner, the therapist helped me see how damaging my codependency was to me as well as to my relationships."

■ **63.** Have you ever had therapy or counseling? If so, have certain problematic patterns in your relationships with other people been pointed out to you in the course of that therapy or counseling? Has a therapist ever discussed with you the concept of codependency and how that dynamic might be affecting your life?

"I always felt so threatened by men. I just assumed they saw me only as a sex object, not as a real person with feelings. For this reason, I was unable to build and maintain genuine friendships with men. Thanks to the lessons I learned in recovery, I am able to see that I have so much more to offer men than my body and sex. Because of my new attitudes and beliefs in recovery, I now have several very good friendships with men."

■ **64.** How do you relate to members of the opposite sex? Do you tend to generalize about members of the opposite sex and, if so, how do you see them: As potential partners? As competition? As friends? As parents?

"Prior to my recovery, I was comfortable only with women who were overweight or who I judged to be not as physically attractive as I. I always felt compelled to compete with other women for the attention of men. Of course, this dynamic adversely affected my friendships with women."

■ **65.**   How do you relate to adults of your same sex?

"*I used to compare myself—particularly my appearance—to every woman I saw or met. I never felt I was thin enough to be acceptable. And regardless of what I was wearing or how self-assured I felt about my appearance, I could always find other women who were dressed more attractively or seductively than I. I compulsively compared myself to women with red hair because I knew that my partner liked red hair.*"

■ **66.** Do you spend time comparing yourself to others physically, financially, intellectually, or sexually?

"At parties, I always paid a great deal of attention to one or two women who I felt were prettier than I and who were being particularly friendly toward my partner as well. I would keep my eyes on these women throughout the evening, mentally listing all the ways they appeared to be better than I."

■ **67.** Do you pick people out of crowds whom you believe your partner will be attracted to? If so, how do you feel toward these people?

"As a codependent, I held the erroneous belief that I had the power to make my partner happy and keep him happy as well. Therefore, whenever he was anything other than happy, I'd give him a gift, wear something sexy, or think up some new sexual game."

■**68.** Do you try to keep your partner from feeling sad, angry, or bored? If so, how do you attempt to do this?

"My partner seemed to be unhappy so much of the time. As a codependent, I assumed that his unhappiness must be my fault in some way and that I had the power to do something about it. I feared that if I didn't do something about his blue moods, he might leave me or have an affair. I believed that the perfect treatment for his unhappiness was for me to have sex with him."

■ **69.** What are you afraid will happen if your partner feels unhappy?

"*I realize now that when my partner would return home after acting out with someone else, he would be unusually nice to me, but he also seemed unable to look me in the eye and he seemed to prefer being alone. Whenever I was uncertain about what he'd been doing, I'd carefully watch him for clues that he had been with another woman. Many codependents claim that they* just knew *when their partners had been acting out— through ESP, intuition, or what might be referred to as a kind of 'codependent radar.'*"

■ **70.** In what ways did you "know" that your partner was acting out his or her sex addiction?

Unmanageability

The twenty-nine questions that follow in this section relate to the element of unmanageability in the codependent's life.

"Unmanageability is the price we pay for our addiction—the things we do and don't do because of our obsession with the sex addict(s) in our lives. To me, unmanageability meant that all areas of my life were out of control. My feelings absolutely overwhelmed me and my behaviors were extreme. I feared that my partner was acting out and would leave me, and I was lonely and angry much of the time. I was either eating everything in sight to console myself or I was not eating anything at all, in a desperate effort to lose weight. When my partner was away, I was abusing drugs. I was either compulsive about house cleaning or I lived in a mess."

■ **71.** What does unmanageability mean to you? In what ways is your life unmanageable now?

"As a codependent, I constantly put the needs of my partner ahead of the needs of anyone else in my life. For example, when my sister got married, she asked me to be her maid of honor and spend the day of her wedding with her. But I was so concerned with making sure that my partner wasn't bored, that I all but ignored my sister on her special day."

■**72.** Have your family and friends been affected by your compulsive attention to the addict(s) in your life?

"From a very early age, I had planned to attend medical school. But my college grades suffered so much because of my preoccupation with finding just the right man; in fact, my grade point average provided me with a ready excuse to not apply to medical school at all. And by not applying to medical school, I was able to justify staying in the small town where my partner was still in school."

■ **73.** Has your education been affected by your codependent behaviors? In what ways? How does knowledge of this make you feel?

"Because of the limitations of the training I received in my field, I settled for part-time work that I was basically overqualified for. I finally 'dared' to apply to medical school and begin my degree program ten years later and five years into my recovery."

■**74.** Has your career been affected by your codependent behaviors? In what ways? How does knowledge of this make you feel?

*"At one time in my relationship with my partner, I was
offered an excellent job in my field that would have required that I spend a year in another city for training.
But I turned down this opportunity and kept my two
part-time minimum-wage jobs because I knew that my
partner would not remain faithful to me while I was
away."*

■**75.** Has your financial well-being been affected by
your codependent behaviors? In what ways? How does
knowledge of this make you feel?

"Early in our relationship, my partner and I were having intercourse so often that I was injured. Despite the pain, however, I never said no to sex with him and I never told him how terribly painful intercourse was for me. I was afraid that if I were to be honest with him about my pain, he would just find another sex partner. Eventually, I had to have surgery for my injuries related to sexual activity. Even during the time that I was supposed to be healing from this surgery, we had intercourse. This untimely sexual activity ultimately caused some permanent scarring which is still painful to me now, years later."

■**76.** Do you suffer from physical pain or other symptoms as a direct result of your codependency? Describe the circumstances and your feelings.

"In some ways, I truly believe that I made my partner my Higher Power. After all, I made him—and therefore his addiction—the center of my life. Furthermore, I was afraid to be open with my partner about my spiritual beliefs; I was fearful that he would think my beliefs were silly."

■ **77.** Has your codependency affected your spirituality? In what ways? How does the knowledge of this make you feel?

"In college, I spent virtually all of my time with my part-ner, so I lost contact with my college friends. My grades also suffered because I spent so little time studying."

■ **78.** Have you sacrificed certain things—other rela-tionships, goals, objectives—because of your commit-ment of time and energy to an addict?

"I met my partner in college and subsequently gave up all plans to leave the state to go to graduate school. I wanted to stay with him—even though he was engaged to someone else at the time! The following justifications sound familiar to many codependents: 'Love is more important than career or money; I probably wouldn't have succeeded anyway.' "

■**79.** Have you given up any dreams, aspirations, or hopes for your own life in order to be in a relationship with an addict? How have you justified to yourself that this person is really worth what you gave up?

━━━━

"When my partner didn't show up to meet me at a party one time, I drank until I passed out. The next morning, I woke up in bed with two men I didn't even know. Word of this got around campus; consequently I was labeled a 'party girl.' Looking back, many codependents realize how their codependent behaviors directly affected their reputations."

■**80.** Do you sense or know for a fact that your codependent behavior has affected your reputation in a negative way? If so, how do you feel about this?

*"It seemed that whenever my partner would suggest a
sexual activity that I didn't enjoy or that I actually
found offensive, I would protest. But then, when he'd
simply say that I was sexually uptight, I'd overlook my
preferences and sometimes even disregard my values
so that I could please him and take part in the
activity."*

■**81.** Have you been called "old-fashioned," or have you
been told that you have a "hang-up" when you've set
sexual boundaries or limits? If so, how did that feel to
you and how did you respond?

"My partner seemed to enjoy it when I was vocal during sex and I tried not to disappoint him. One time, I overheard his neighbors laughing and joking about how noisy I was during sex. Although these people were friends, I was very uncomfortable around them after that."

■**82.** Has your sexual behavior caused embarrassment for you in front of others? Try to give one example and pay particular attention to your feelings at that time and now.

"Prior to my recovery, all touch seemed sexual to me. Now, in recovery, I am able to ask for hugs from my partner when I am sad or afraid. With both of us in recovery, we have learned that we can, indeed, touch each other without that touch necessarily leading to intercourse. And when we do have sex, I ask for what I want and I feel free to state clearly what I don't want."

■ **83.** What kind of touch—sexual and nonsexual—do you like? How do you make these preferences known to your partner?

"When I met my partner, I told him that I liked sex a lot. But at that time, I was accepting quantity rather than quality. I realize now that what I really wanted was a man to hold me and tell me that he cared about me. Now, in recovery, my partner and I have sex less often, but we enjoy it more. We enjoy sex more because we no longer use it in an effort to get close; we are sexual with each other to enhance an emotional intimacy between us that already exists."

■**84.** Do you enjoy having sex with your partner?

"In the early days of our acting-out behaviors, I was very active in initiating sexual activity. I believed this would hold his attraction and help maintain the relationship."

■**85.**   Are you active or passive when it comes to sexual activity with your partner? Does your role feel right and comfortable to you? Are you denying some of your wants and needs by taking on a certain role in your relationship?

"Some codependents have come to dread sex because they find it emotionally or physically painful or because the activity conjures up unpleasant feelings or painful memories."

■**86.** At this time in your life, do you dread having sex? If so, what do you think the reasons are?

*"Regardless of how painful sex was for me—emotion-
ally or physically—I never said anything to my partner about it. I was afraid that if I mentioned anything
about my own difficulties to him, he'd just leave me to
have sex with someone else."*

■ **87.** Has sex ever been painful for you? If so, what did
you do about it? Did you tell your partner? If so, what
was his or her reaction?

"I always felt so numb after having sex. My only interest was in making sure that he was happy."

■**88.** How do you usually feel after having sex?

"It seems as though before my recovery, I spent all of my free time cleaning and organizing the house. When my partner was home, this activity made me essentially unavailable to be sexual with him; when he was gone, this compulsive cleaning activity helped to distract me somewhat from thinking about what he might be doing while he was away."

■ **89.** Are you compulsively involved in certain activities in an effort to numb, deny, or forget the pain of your relationship? Name these activities and how you have used them in this way.

"In my efforts to accommodate my partner's sexual drive, I once suggested to him that we place an ad in the newspaper in order to find people who would be sexual with us. So after only brief phone conversations with people answering the ad, we invited these absolute strangers into our home and engaged in sexual activities with them. In order to take part in these activities, I completely repressed my fears about disease and violence."

■**90.** In what ways has your codependent behavior interfered with your own judgment or standards?

"My partner would oftentimes spend the weekend at his parent's cabin. I was sure that he was really spending that time with another woman. During the times he was away, I'd go to a friend's house—there I'd drink alcohol and smoke marijuana all day and night so I wouldn't think about what my partner might be doing. When my partner and I were together, I rarely used alcohol or other drugs."

■**91.** Do you use or abuse alcohol and/or other drugs? Do you feel that your use/abuse of these substances is related to your codependency in any way?

"Whenever my partner was late for dinner, I'd be afraid he was acting out sexually somewhere. I'd eat my meal alone, then sit down with a box of cookies and devour the whole thing—without so much as giving it a thought. Then I'd feel so bad and nauseous that I'd just go to bed, no matter what time it was. Many codependents say that they have used food as an escape rather than for nutrition."

■**92.** What role does food play in your life?

"A friend of mine once told me that she had seen my partner kissing a woman in a hotel lobby. I told her that it couldn't have been him because he was always working at that time of day. I never asked him about it; months later, I found out that he often met women at that hotel during the day."

■ **93.** Have you denied or otherwise avoided believing facts about the acting-out behaviors of your partner? Cite a situation in which you did this.

"*One time when my partner and I were at a party together, he and another woman went outside to talk. I was sure that this was one of the women he had slept with. My response? I poured myself a strong drink and sat on a man's lap, just hoping that my partner would notice me, get jealous, and stay where I could keep an eye on him for the rest of the evening. When we got home that night, I fought with my partner about what he had worn to the party rather than telling him how upset I was about him being alone with another woman while we were there.*

"*Many codependents speak of having used one or all of the following 'coping mechanisms' when they suspected their partners of acting out: interrogation, ignoring the signs or facts, putting all their energies into proving it, trying to counter by doing things that they believed would make their partners jealous.*"

■ **94.** List some things you have done to "cope" at times when you knew or suspected that your partner was acting out sexually.

"Even before we were married, I seemed to have an uncontrollable need to stop by my partner's apartment, unannounced, at all times of the day and night. If he wasn't there, I'd call his family. If he wasn't with his family, I felt sure that he was with another woman. Some codependents speak of violating their own codes of behavior by looking at their partners' datebooks, financial records, and mail in an effort to check up on their activities."

■**95.** In what ways have you "checked up" on your partner? How did you feel doing this and how important was it to you to find the truth about his or her activities?

"I felt that if I were more sexually satisfying to my part-
ner, he wouldn't need other women and I would be
enough for him. As summer approached each year, I
was extremely tough on myself about losing weight. I
thought if I got a sexy new swimsuit, he'd keep his eyes
on me instead of looking at other women. Many code-
pendents erroneously believe that they can actually
stop their partners from acting out by changing some-
thing about themselves: getting a better education,
having a baby, wearing more or less makeup, having
cosmetic surgery, making more money."

■ **96.** Have you thought to yourself that you could stop
your partner's acting-out behaviors by changing something about yourself? What things about yourself have
you changed or considered changing in an effort to control your partner?

"When I met my partner, I already knew that he 'slept around.' In fact, our relationship began that way. I felt that I had no right to expect him to change for me, even when we got married. I told myself that if I wasn't so old-fashioned, I would be able to accept this. When we codependents to sex addicts compare notes, we realize that at one time or another, we all used the same phrases to 'explain'—to ourselves and others—the acting-out behaviors of our partners: 'I guess I shouldn't worry, almost everyone strays from time to time.' 'After all, it only happened once.' 'It's only a phase he/she is going through.' 'My partner is unable to be monogamous; I knew that about him/her when we married, so I really have no right to expect a major change now.' "

■ **97.**   Have you tried to minimize, rationalize or justify the acting-out behaviors of your partner?

"I found myself saying things like this about my partner and his acting-out behavior: 'It's not his fault, she threw herself at him; their affair is her fault.'"

■ **98.** How have you focused your anger on *whom* your partner acted out with rather than on your partner's behavior itself?

—

"Due to my obsession with the addict in my life, I was depressed and unable to find joy in anything I did. I had given up all of my hobbies and all of my friends in order to focus all of my attention on him. Then, one day, I realized that my life was becoming a replay of my mother's life—feeling trapped in one empty and abusive relationship after another. It was then that I finally understood that in my codependency, I had completely lost myself. I decided that it was more important to reclaim myself than to live the lie that a bad relationship is better than no relationship at all.

These considerations are sometimes called 'hitting bottom'—a point at which a person decides that change—though filled with uncertainty and risk—is less painful than continuing to live as one is living. In some cases, this point is marked by a crisis such as a divorce, a suicide attempt, discovery of another affair, loss of a job, loss of an important relationship, or an emotional breakdown."

■ **99.** What would have to take place in your life in order to convince you that you cannot go on living the way you have been living?

■ **100.** What has *already taken place* in your life that convinces you that you cannot go on living the way you have been living?

Once you have an emotional acceptance of the First Step, you are ready to move on to the other eleven steps and the journey to recovery. Accepting your powerlessness signals the beginning of recovery; the other steps will be equally important to you as you continue on in your recovery.

Jem: "I encourage you to save this workbook so that you can refer back to it at various stages in your recovery. It will help you recall the impact that codependency has had on your life whenever defense mechanisms threaten to become operative again. This workbook and your very personal responses in it will also show you clearly how far your recovery has progressed at times when you might be doubting that things are getting better. Trust me: many times in your recovery, you will find it a very moving experience to look back at your original First Step, a good portion of which is now recorded in this workbook."

Both of us offer our encouragement to you as you continue on the journey of recovery; both of us wish you well in your growth.

Mic Hunter
and
Jem

Resources

■

A primary resource for codependents to sex addicts is a Twelve Step fellowship based on the Twelve Step Program of Alcoholics Anonymous. If you are already affiliated with this kind of fellowship, be sure to draw on the help and support it provides as you work the First Step and each of the eleven steps that follow.

Because the First Step process brings up so many memories and emotions, it would be wise for you to talk with your Twelve Step Program sponsor and other group members about your First Step. In fact, you may want to use some of the questions in this workbook as topics for discussion at Twelve Step meetings.

If you are not yet affiliated with a Twelve Step recovery program, we encourage you to do several things:

- Be persistent in your search for a Twelve Step group. Because the Twelve Step Program is anonymous in nature and bases its public relations activities on the principle of attraction rather than promotion, your initial efforts to gather information about the Program and specific groups and meetings may not be successful. For information regarding anonymous groups based on the Twelve Step Program in your area, you may find it helpful to check the phone book or consult with a social service agency or a community mental health referral service. Since 1983, awareness of sex addiction and codependency has steadily grown; currently, there are Twelve Step groups for sex addicts throughout the country and there are growing numbers of Twelve Step groups for codependents to sex addicts.

- If you are unable to find a Twelve Step group in your community that is appropriate for your needs, arrange to attend other Twelve Step group meetings and talk with people there about establishing a special Twelve Step group to address the needs of codependents to sex addicts.

- Whenever possible, ask recovering codependents to share their personal stories with you—particularly how they came to see their powerlessness and how they are progressing in their recovery. Don't hesitate to discuss the Twelve Steps with other recovering people and always try to consider the many ways you can use the Twelve Steps in your daily life.

- *Most important, be patient and gentle with yourself.*

Recommended Reading

■

Anonymous. *Alcoholics Anonymous*. New York: A.A. World Services. 1976 (© 1939).

_____ . *Twelve Steps and Twelve Traditions*. New York: A.A. World Services, 11th printing, 1972, (© 1953).

Carnes, Patrick. *Out of the Shadows: Understanding Sexual Addiction*. Minneapolis: CompCare Publishers. 1983.

_____ . *Contrary to Love: Helping the Sexual Addict*. Minneapolis: CompCare Publishers. 1989.

Fossum, M. and M. Mason. *Facing Shame: Families in Recovery*. New York: W.W. Norton & Company. 1986.

Grateful Members (Anonymous). *The Twelve Steps for Everyone . . . who really wants them*. Minneapolis: CompCare. 1977.

Halpern, Howard. *How to Break Your Addiction to a Person*. New York: Bantam. 1982.

Hunter, Mic. *The Twelve Steps and Shame*. Center City: Hazelden Foundation. 1988.

_____ . *What Is Sex Addiction?* Center City: Hazelden Foundation. 1988.

Kasl, Charlotte. *Women, Sex and Addiction: A Search for Love and Power*. New York: Ticknor & Fields. 1989.

LeSourd, Sandra Simpson. *The Compulsive Woman*. New Jersey: Chosen Books. 1987.

Nelson, James. *Embodiment: An Approach to Sexuality and Christian Theology*. New York: The Pilgrim Press. 1978.

P.D.N.E.C. (Anonymous). *Hope and Recovery: A Twelve Step guide for healing from compulsive sexual behavior*. Minneapolis: CompCare. 1987. (Portions of this book dealing with the Twelve Steps and Twelve Traditions are also available on audio cassette.)

————— . *What Everyone Needs to Know about Sex Addiction.* Minneapolis: CompCare. 1989.

Peele, Stanton. *Love & Addiction.* New York: New American Library. 1975.

About the Authors

■

Mic Hunter practices in St. Paul, Minnesota, where his clients include codependents and other people whose lives are affected by compulsive behaviors. Prior to working in mental health clinics, Hunter worked with several chemical dependency treatment programs. He has a master's degree in human development and a master's degree in education/psychological services. He has also completed two specialized programs at the University of Minnesota: the Alcohol/Drug Education Counseling Program and the Chemical Dependency and Family Intimacy Training Project of the Program in Human Sexuality. He is certified as a Chemical Dependency Counselor (Reciprocal) and is licensed as a Psychologist. Hunter is also author of *The Twelve Steps and Shame* and *What Is Sex Addiction?*.

Jem is a recovering codependent to sex addicts.